101

To Do With Chocolate

BY
STEPHANIE
ASHCRAFT

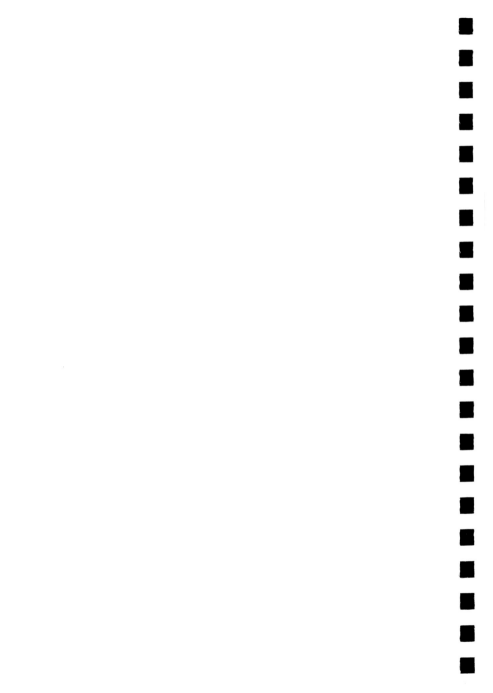

101 Things To Do With Chocolate

101 Things To Do With Chocolate

BY
STEPHANIE ASHCRAFT

Gibbs Smith, Publisher
TO ENRICH AND INSPIRE HUMANKIND
Salt Lake City | Charleston | Santa Fe | Santa Barbara

First Edition
12 11 10 09 08   20 19 18 17 16 15 14 13 12 11 10 9 8 7 6 5 4 3 2

Published by
Gibbs Smith, Publisher
P.O. Box 667
Layton, Utah 84041

Orders: 1.800.835.4993
www.gibbs-smith.com

Printed and bound in Korea

Library of Congress Cataloging-in-Publication Data
Ashcraft, Stephanie.
  101 things to do with chocolate / Stephanie Ashcraft.
     p. cm.
  ISBN-13: 978-1-4236-0180-7
  ISBN-10: 1-4236-0180-7
  1. Cookery (Chocolate) 2. Desserts. I. Title. II. Title: One hundred and one things to do
with chocolate.

TX767.C5A74 2007
641.6'374—dc22
                              2007029135

To all my family in Indiana and Illinois,
thank you for always loving and encouraging
me in all that I do.

To all my Ashcraft family, thank you for
allowing me to be your "favorite" aunt and
sister-in-law. You're all my favorites, too.

To my parents, thank you for teaching
me correct principles and giving me the
room and direction to fly.

I love you all.

CONTENTS

Helpful Hints 9

Candies
Easy Holiday Mint Truffles 12 • Peanut Butter Chocolate Candy 13 • Decadent Chocolate Truffles 14 • Cream Cheese Truffles 15 • Fun-Topped Fudge 16 • Brown Family Orange Sticks 17 • Chocolate-Coated Cookie Balls 18 • Chocolate Butter Nut Crunch 19 • Rocky Road Drops 20

Cookies
Vanilla Chocolate Chip Cookies 22 • Coconut Cream Chocolate Chip Cookies 23 • Chocolate Butter Pecan Cookies 24 • Nutty Chocolate Chip Cereal Cookies 25 • Oatmeal Chocolate Chip Cookies 26 • Peanut Butter Chocolate Chip Cookies 27 • No-Bake Chocolate Drops 28 • Macadamia Nut Chocolate Cookies 29 • Pumpkin Chocolate Chip Cookies 30 • Chocolate Chunk Cookies 31 • Chocolate Chip Cookies 32 • Chocolate Chip Pudding Sandwich Cookies 33 • Peanut Butter Candy Cookies 34 • Rolo Surprise Cookies 35

Brownies
Pink Peppermint Frosted Brownies 38 • Rocky Road Brownies 39 • Doctored-Up Brownies 40 • Cookie Dough Brownies 41 • Easy Brownies from Scratch 42 • Caramel Cashew Brownies 43 • Chocolate Mint Layer Brownies 44 • Peanut Butter Cup Brownies 45

Bars
Chocolate Caramel Candy Bars 48 • Chocolate Peanut Layer Bars 49 • Peanut Butter Chip Cookie Bars 50 • Chocolate Fall Harvest Bars 51 • Chocolate Peanut Butter Fantasy Bars 52 • Decadent Semisweet Cookie Bars 53 • Chocolate Layer Bars 54 • Chocolate Cream Cheese Bars 55 • Peanut Butter Crunch Bars 56 • Chocolate Chip Pudding Bars 57 • White Chocolate Almond Bars 58 • Chocolate Cheesecake Bars 59 • Hello Dollies 60

Cakes & Bundt Cakes

Double-Chocolate Almond Cake 62 • Banana Chocolate Chip Cake 63 • Blackberry Chocolate Cake 64 • Chocolate Peanut Butter Cake 65 • Entertaining Delight Cake 66 • Butterfinger Sheet Cake 67 • Moist Chocolate Mayonnaise Cake 68 • Chocolate Peanut Butter Candy Cake 69 • Cherry-Chocolate Bundt Cake 70 • Sweet-Glazed Chocolate Bundt Cake 71

Ice Cream Cakes & Sandwiches

Colorful Ice Cream Sandwiches 74 • Grasshopper Ice Cream Sandwiches 75 • Nutty Chocolate Chip Ice Cream Sandwiches 76 • Brownie Ice Cream Cake 77 • Instant Ice Cream Sandwich Cake 78 • Cookie Dough Ice Cream Cake 79 • Cookies-and-Cream Ice Cream Cake 80 • Mint Chocolate Chip Ice Cream Cake 81 • Peanut Butter Chocolate Ice Cream Cake 82 • Rocky Road Ice Cream Cake 83

Cheesecakes, Dessert Pizzas, & Pies

Candy Bar Cheesecake 86 • Chocolate Chip Cheesecake 87 • Fudge Truffle Cheesecake 88 • Chocolate Strawberry Cheesecake Bars 89 • Coconut Almond Pizza 90 • Banana Split Pizza 91 • Chocolate Chip Cookie Pizza 92 • Candy Bar Pudding Pie 93 • Chocolate Mousse Pie 94 • Cookies-and-Cream Ice Cream Pie 95

Family Favorites

Hot Chocolate 98 • Cookies-and-Cream Milkshake 99 • No-Bake Peanut Butter Oatmeal Squares 100 • Chocolate Cream Cheese Cupcakes 101 • Chocolate Peanut Butter Surprise Cupcakes 102 • Chocolate-Covered Cereal Squares 103 • Butterscotch Chocolate Crispy Squares 104 • Chocolate Lush 105 • Graham Cracker Chocolate Squares 106 • Peanut Butter Chocolate Crispy Treats 107 • Chocolate Chip Banana Bread 108 • Peanut Butter Chocolate Squares 109 • Oatmeal Caramelitos 110 • Chocolate Pudding-Filled Donuts 111 • Chocolate Graham Cracker Cake 112

Trifles & Entertaining Ideas

Cookies-and-Cream Trifle 114 • Mint Brownie Trifle 115 • Butterfinger Brownie a la Mode 116 • Mint Chocolate Chip Brownie Sundaes 117 • Chocolate Lovers Parfaits 118 • Raspberry Brownie Cups 119 • Peanut Butter Cookie Cups 120 • Peanut Butter Chocolate Lush 121 • Chocolate-Dipped Strawberries 122 • Chocolate-Covered Pretzels 123 • Berry Chocolate Bars 124 • Cream Puff Squares 125

HELPFUL HINTS

1. Remember that chocolate can be easily scorched or ruined. Whether melting chocolate in a heavy pan, double boiler, slow cooker, or microwave, gently heat chocolate, stirring frequently until melted. Never leave melting chocolate unattended; it will burn if not watched carefully. Avoid getting any water in the chocolate, as water will create clumps. If this happens, add 1 teaspoon to 1 tablespoon shortening to the chocolate and stir until smooth.

2. Melting chocolate can be done in the microwave as well. Make sure the microwave-safe dish you are using is completely dry. Microwave 1 cup chocolate chips on high for 45 seconds. Chocolate should be half melted. If not, microwave an additional 30 seconds. Remove and stir until chocolate lumps melt completely.

3. Dipping chocolate is one of my family's favorite things to do. When I am ready to dip, I melt my chocolate in the slow cooker. The chocolate can be left on low heat, stirring occasionally to break up any chocolate lumps. You can take your time dipping with this method. With other methods, you have to hurry to use the chocolate before it hardens again.

4. It can be easy to make chocolate candy. Many craft stores sell candy molds and chocolate candy melts. Heat the candy melts in a small slow cooker on high heat. Once melted, turn heat to low. Spoon chocolate into ungreased molds. Tap filled molds on the table to remove any air bubbles. Place molds in the freezer 15 minutes or until chocolate is hard. If making suckers, be sure to place the sucker stick in the chocolate and then give it a full twist to assure it will stay in the sucker.

5. Store chocolate in a covered or an airtight container in a cool, dry place, such as the refrigerator or freezer. If storing in the refrigerator or freezer, allow chocolate to come to room temperature before adding it to a recipe.

6. Chocolate will sometimes start to turn gray on the outside, especially when it becomes too warm. The chocolate is still good and will return to its natural color once melted.

7. Milk chocolate chips can be used in place of semisweet chips in any recipe. Milk chocolate chips are sweeter and creamier than semisweet chips, but semisweet chocolate adds a rich, more dense chocolate taste to recipes.

8. My favorite chocolate cake mix is Betty Crocker's Triple Chocolate Fudge. It can be used in any recipe calling for a chocolate cake mix.

9. Always grease and flour the cake pan or spray it with oil—even when the recipe doesn't call for it.

10. Bake cakes on the middle oven rack, never on the top or bottom racks.

11. For best results, use glass or stoneware baking dishes.

12. For chewier cookies and bars, take them out of the oven just as they begin to turn golden brown around the edges and let them cool on or in the pan.

CANDIES

EASY HOLIDAY
MINT TRUFFLES

2/3 cup **whipping cream**
1 bag (11.5 ounces) **semisweet chocolate chips**
1 to 1 1/2 teaspoons **mint extract**
**sweetened coconut flakes,
chopped chocolate chips, chopped
mint chips or Andes Mints, or
chopped candy canes for topping**

In a saucepan, heat whipping cream until it starts to boil. Remove from heat; immediately stir in chocolate chips and mint extract. Stir until chips melt completely. Pour into a medium bowl. Cover with plastic wrap and refrigerate 2–3 hours, or until firm.

Line a baking sheet with wax paper. Drop heaping teaspoons of chocolate mixture onto wax paper. Place baking sheet in freezer and freeze chocolates 40–50 minutes. Place desired toppings in separate bowls. Shape frozen truffles into 1-inch balls and then roll in toppings. Cover and refrigerate 2 hours. Store truffles in an airtight container in the refrigerator. Makes 20 truffles.

PEANUT BUTTER
CHOCOLATE CANDY

I cup	**crunchy or creamy peanut butter**
$^1/_2$ cup	**butter or margarine,** melted
3$^1/_2$ cups	**powdered sugar**
I bag (11.5 ounces)	**chocolate chips**

In a large bowl, combine peanut butter and butter. Stir in powdered sugar. Knead with hands until powdered sugar is worked completely into peanut butter mixture. Refrigerate if not being used immediately.

Form peanut butter dough into small balls about 1-inch in diameter and place on wax paper. Melt chocolate chips in a microwave-safe dish, stirring every 30 seconds until smooth. Roll balls in chocolate and place back onto wax paper. Refrigerate at least I hour, or until chocolate hardens. Makes 30–35 candies.

DECADENT
CHOCOLATE TRUFFLES

2 cups	**semisweet chocolate chips**
I cup	**milk chocolate chips**
I can (14 ounces)	**sweetened condensed milk**
I tablespoon	**vanilla**
	finely chopped nuts, sweetened coconut flakes, cake decorating sprinkles, powdered sugar, or cocoa powder for topping

In a heavy 2-quart pan, melt together chocolate chips and condensed milk; stir in vanilla. Refrigerate 2 or more hours in the pan until firm.

Place desired toppings in separate bowls. Shape chocolate into small balls about 1-inch in diameter and then roll in toppings. Store in the refrigerator until ready to serve. Makes 35 truffles.

CREAM CHEESE TRUFFLES

I package (8 ounces)	**cream cheese,** softened
3 cups	**powdered sugar,** sifted
2 cups	**milk chocolate chips**
I cup	**semisweet chocolate chips**
I tablespoon	**vanilla**
	finely chopped nuts, sweetened coconut flakes, cake decorating sprinkles, powdered sugar, or cocoa for topping

In a bowl, combine cream cheese and powdered sugar with a hand mixer until smooth. Melt chocolate chips together and then stir melted chocolate and vanilla into powdered sugar mixture until it turns an even brown color. Refrigerate 2 hours.

Place desired toppings in separate bowls. Shape chocolate into small balls about I-inch in diameter and then roll in toppings. Makes 40 truffles.

VARIATION: Use I cup peanut butter chips in place of semisweet chocolate chips.

FUN-TOPPED FUDGE

4 1/2 cups **sugar**
I can (12 ounces) **evaporated milk**
1/2 cup **butter or margarine,** melted
I bag (11.5 ounces) **semisweet chocolate chips**
I jar (7 ounces) **marshmallow creme**
3/4 cup **chopped nuts, crushed**
Butterfinger, crushed candy cane,
mint baking chips, or mini
M&M's for topping

In a nonstick pan, bring sugar, milk, and butter to a boil. Boil 6–8 minutes, stirring constantly. Turn off heat and stir in chocolate chips and marshmallow creme. Spread fudge evenly into a greased 8 x 8-inch or 9 x 9-inch pan. Chill at least I hour before sprinkling toppings over top. Lightly press topping into fudge; refrigerate overnight. Makes 16–20 servings.

BROWN FAMILY ORANGE STICKS

2 cups **water**
2 cups **sugar**
2 **oranges**
2 bars (5 each ounces) **dark chocolate**

In a 3-quart saucepan, boil together water and sugar over medium heat. While waiting for mixture to boil, use a knife or orange peeler to remove the peel in four even sections for each orange, thick peel works the best; discard oranges. Cut each section into five long slices about $1/4$-inch thick. Orange peel slices will be about the same size as thin french fries.

Once mixture begins to boil, add orange peel slices and lightly boil for 10 minutes, or until the orange peels are saturated with the sugar. Orange peels will become translucent. Strain the peels and set aside.

Break bars of chocolate into small pieces and place in a small slow cooker. Stir chocolate over high heat until it melts; turn heat to low. Using a fork or toothpick, dip each orange peel slice into the melted chocolate until coated completely. Lay chocolate orange sticks on wax paper placed on a baking sheet. Place pan in freezer for 15 minutes to harden chocolate. Store in the refrigerator. Makes 35–40 chocolate orange sticks.

CHOCOLATE-COATED COOKIE BALLS

1 bag (1 pound) **chocolate sandwich cookies,**
chopped
1 package (8 ounces) **cream cheese,** softened
20 ounces **chocolate almond bark,** melted

In a large bowl, combine chopped cookies and cream cheese to form
dough. Roll into small balls about 1 to 1 1/2-inches in diameter. Using a
fork, dip balls into melted chocolate. Set balls on wax paper and chill 1
hour, or until set. Makes 35–40 candies.

VARIATIONS: Use chocolate mint sandwich cookies, chocolate peanut
butter filled sandwich cookies, or any other variation of sandwich cookies.

CHOCOLATE BUTTER NUT CRUNCH

1 cup **sugar**
$^1/_4$ cup **water**
$^1/_2$ cup **butter or margarine**
$^1/_2$ teaspoon **salt**
1$^1/_2$ cups **chocolate chips**
$^1/_2$ cup **finely chopped nuts**

In a 2-quart nonstick pan, combine sugar, water, butter, and salt. Boil until mixture reaches 290 degrees on a candy thermometer. Pour onto a greased baking sheet and let cool.

In the microwave, melt half the chocolate chips 45–60 seconds. Stir and spread chocolate over hardened candy. Sprinkle half the nuts over top. Place baking sheet in freezer 20 minutes and allow chocolate to harden; flip candy. Melt remaining chocolate chips and spread over uncovered side of candy. Sprinkle remaining nuts over top. Freeze an additional 20 minutes. Once chocolate hardens, break candy into pieces. Makes 8–10 servings.

ROCKY ROAD DROPS

2 cups **milk chocolate chips**
1 can (14 ounces) **sweetened condensed milk**
3 1/2 cups **miniature marshmallows**
2 1/2 cups **salted dry roasted peanuts**

In a heavy saucepan, melt chocolate with condensed milk over low heat. Once chocolate is completely melted and smooth, remove from heat.

In a large bowl, combine marshmallows and nuts. Stir in chocolate mixture. Drop by spoonfuls onto wax paper and then refrigerate 2 hours, or until set. Makes 36–45 drops.

Cookies

VANILLA CHOCOLATE CHIP COOKIES

I cup	**butter or margarine,** softened
3/4 cup	**brown sugar**
1/4 cup	**sugar**
I small box	**vanilla instant pudding mix**
2	**eggs**
I teaspoon	**vanilla**
2 1/4 cups	**flour**
I teaspoon	**baking soda**
1/4 teaspoon	**salt**
3/4 cup	**semisweet chocolate chips**
I 1/4 cups	**milk chocolate chips**

Preheat oven to 350 degrees.

In a large bowl, combine butter, brown sugar, and sugar. Stir in pudding mix, eggs, and vanilla.

In a separate bowl, combine flour, baking soda, and salt. Slowly stir flour mixture into pudding mixture. Stir in chocolate chips. Drop heaping teaspoons of dough onto a greased baking sheet. Bake 10–12 minutes, or until lightly golden around the edges. Makes 36 cookies.

COCONUT CREAM CHOCOLATE CHIP COOKIES

2¹/₄ cups	**flour**
I teaspoon	**baking soda**
I cup	**butter or margarine,** softened
¹/₄ cup	**sugar**
³/₄ cup	**brown sugar**
I teaspoon	**vanilla**
I small box	**coconut cream instant pudding mix**
2	**eggs**
I¹/₂ cups	**semisweet chocolate chips**
I cup	**coconut**

Preheat oven to 375 degrees.

In a medium bowl, combine flour and baking soda.

In a large bowl, combine butter, sugar, brown sugar, and vanilla; mix until smooth. Beat in pudding mix and eggs. Slowly stir in flour mixture followed by chocolate chips and coconut. Drop heaping teaspoons of dough onto a greased baking sheet. Bake 9–10 minutes, or until lightly golden around the edges. Makes 36 cookies.

CHOCOLATE BUTTER PECAN COOKIES

1 **chocolate cake mix**
2 **eggs**
$^1/_2$ cup **butter or margarine,** melted
1 container (15 ounces) **coconut pecan frosting**

Preheat oven to 350 degrees.

In a bowl, mix cake mix, eggs, butter, and frosting together until smooth. Refrigerate dough 1–2 hours. Drop heaping teaspoons of dough onto a lightly greased baking sheet. Bake 10–12 minutes. Remove from pan and place cookies on a nonstick cooling rack. Makes 36 cookies.

NUTTY CHOCOLATE CHIP CEREAL COOKIES

²/₃ cup	**butter-flavored shortening**
¹/₂ cup	**brown sugar,** firmly packed
2	**eggs**
1	**chocolate cake mix**
1 cup	**crispy rice cereal**
1 cup	**white, semisweet, or milk chocolate chips**
¹/₂ cup	**chopped nuts**

Preheat oven to 350 degrees.

In a bowl, blend shortening and brown sugar together. Beat eggs in one at a time and then stir in cake mix. With a spoon, stir in cereal, chocolate chips and nuts. Drop heaping teaspoons of dough onto a lightly greased baking sheet. Bake 9–12 minutes, or until tops look cracked. Do not over bake. Cool 2–3 minutes on baking sheet and then remove cookies and place on a nonstick cooling rack to cool. Makes 40–45 cookies.

OATMEAL CHOCOLATE CHIP COOKIES

1 cup	**shortening**
$^3/_4$ cup	**brown sugar**
$^3/_4$ cup	**sugar**
1 teaspoon	**vanilla**
2	**eggs**
1 $^1/_2$ cups	**flour**
1 teaspoon	**baking soda**
1 teaspoon	**salt**
1 $^1/_2$ cups	**rolled oats**
1 $^1/_2$ cups	**semisweet chocolate chips**

Preheat oven to 350 degrees.

In a large bowl, combine shortening, sugars, and vanilla. Beat in eggs until thoroughly mixed.

In a separate bowl, combine flour, baking soda, salt, and oats. Stir into creamy mixture and then add chocolate chips. Drop teaspoons of dough onto a greased baking sheet. Bake 10–12 minutes, or until lightly golden around the edges. Makes 36–42 cookies.

PEANUT BUTTER CHOCOLATE CHIP COOKIES

    1 **devil's food cake mix**
    2 **eggs**
¹/₂ cup **butter or margarine,** softened
¹/₂ cup **chunky peanut butter**
  1 cup **chocolate chips**

Preheat oven to 350 degrees.

In a bowl, mix together cake mix, eggs, and butter until dough forms. Stir in peanut butter and chocolate chips. Drop teaspoons of dough onto a lightly greased baking sheet. Bake 10–11 minutes. Remove from pan and cool. Makes 30–36 cookies.

VARIATION: To make bars, spread dough evenly into a lightly greased 9 x 13-inch pan. Bake 18–20 minutes.

NO-BAKE CHOCOLATE DROPS

1 cup **chocolate chips**
$^1/_3$ cup **butter or margarine**
18 large **marshmallows**
$^1/_2$ teaspoon **vanilla**
1 cup **coconut**
2 cups **rolled oats**

In a 3-quart heavy pan, combine chocolate chips, butter, and marshmallows. Stir constantly over medium heat until marshmallows and chocolate are melted; remove pan from heat. Stir in vanilla and then fold in coconut and rolled oats. Drop spoonfuls of mixture onto wax paper and cool before serving. Makes 20 cookies.

MACADAMIA NUT CHOCOLATE COOKIES

1	**chocolate cake mix**
2	**eggs**
1/2 cup	**butter or margarine,** softened
1 cup	**white chocolate chunks or chips**
1/2 cup	**chopped macadamia nuts**

Preheat oven to 350 degrees.

In a bowl, mix together cake mix, eggs, and butter. Mixture should be stiff and all the cake mix should be mixed into the dough. Stir in white chocolate and nuts. Use cookie scoop to drop dough onto an ungreased baking sheet. Bake 10–11 minutes. Remove from pan and place on non-stick cooling rack to cool. Makes 36–40 cookies.

VARIATION: 1 cup semisweet or milk chocolate chips or chunks can be substituted in place of white chocolate.

PUMPKIN CHOCOLATE CHIP COOKIES

1	**yellow or spice cake mix**
1 can (15 ounces)	**solid pack pumpkin**
1 cup	**semisweet or milk chocolate chips**

Preheat oven to 350 degrees.

In a large bowl, mix together cake mix and pumpkin until well blended. Stir in chocolate chips. Drop rounded spoonfuls of dough onto a lightly greased baking sheet. Bake 8–10 minutes. Allow cookies to cool on baking sheet 5 minutes before removing to a wire rack to cool completely. Makes 30–36 cookies.

CHOCOLATE CHUNK COOKIES

1	**chocolate cake mix**
2	**eggs**
1/2 cup	**butter or margarine,** softened
1 cup	**rolled oats**
1/2 cup	**chopped pecans or walnuts**
3/4 cup	**coconut**
3 (1.55 ounces each)	**milk chocolate candy bars,** cut into 1/4- to 1/2-inch chunks

Preheat oven to 350 degrees.

In a bowl, mix together cake mix, eggs, and butter. Mixture should be stiff and all the cake mix should be mixed into the dough. Stir in oats, pecans, coconut, and chocolate chunks. Use cookie scoop to drop dough onto a baking sheet. Bake 10–12 minutes. Remove from pan and place on nonstick cooling rack to cool. Makes 36–40 cookies.

VARIATION: 1 cup semisweet or white chocolate chips can be substituted in place of the chocolate chunks.

CHOCOLATE CHIP COOKIES

1 cup	**brown sugar**
$^1/_2$ cup	**sugar**
1 cup	**shortening, butter, or margarine,** softened
2	**eggs**
1 teaspoon	**vanilla**
$2^1/_2$ cups	**flour**
1 teaspoon	**baking soda**
$^3/_4$ teaspoon	**salt**
1 package (11.5 ounces)	**chocolate chips**

Preheat oven to 350 degrees.

In a large bowl, cream together sugars with shortening or butter. Stir in eggs, one at a time; add vanilla.

In a separate bowl, combine flour, baking soda, and salt. Slowly stir flour mixture into sugar mixture. Stir in chocolate chips. Drop teaspoons of dough onto a baking sheet. Bake 10 minutes, or until lightly golden around the edges. Makes 52–60 cookies.

VARIATION: My great-grandmother would sometimes stir in $1^1/_2$ cups crispy rice cereal to this family-favorite cookie dough.

CHOCOLATE CHIP PUDDING SANDWICH COOKIES

Filling:

1 1/2 cups	**milk**
1/2 cup	**creamy peanut butter**
1 small box	**chocolate instant pudding mix**

Cookies:

1	**white cake mix**
2	**eggs**
1/3 cup	**canola oil**
1 cup	**chocolate chips**

In a 2-quart bowl, whisk together milk and peanut butter. Whisk in chocolate pudding mix and then refrigerate until ready to use.

Preheat oven to 350 degrees.

In a 2-quart bowl, combine cake mix, eggs, and oil until cookie dough forms. Stir in chocolate chips. Drop teaspoons of dough onto a baking sheet. Bake 8–11 minutes, or until lightly golden around the edges. Do not over cook. Allow cookies to cool. Place a scoop of pudding mixture between two cookies. Store in refrigerator. Makes 15–18 sandwich cookies.

VARIATION: For peanut butter cookies, stir in 1/2 cup peanut butter into cookie dough before baking.

PEANUT BUTTER
CANDY COOKIES

1 **chocolate cake mix**
2 **eggs**
$^1/_2$ cup **butter or margarine,** softened
$^1/_2$ cup **crunchy peanut butter**
1 to 1$^1/_2$ cups **plain M&M's**

Preheat oven to 350 degrees.

In a large bowl, mix together cake mix, eggs, butter, and peanut butter until cake mix is thoroughly moistened. Stir M&M's into dough. Use a cookie scoop to drop dough onto a baking sheet. Bake 9–12 minutes. Allow cookies to set up on hot baking sheet 2–3 minutes. Remove from pan and place on nonstick cooling rack to cool. Makes 36 cookies.

ROLO SURPRISE COOKIES

1	**white or chocolate cake mix**
2	**eggs**
1/2 cup	**butter or margarine,** softened
36	**individual Rolo candies,** unwrapped

Heat oven to 350 degrees.

In a bowl, mix together cake mix, eggs, and butter until cake mix is thoroughly moistened. Place a Rolo candy in the center of a teaspoon of dough. Roll dough around candy making sure the candy is completely covered with dough. Place onto a baking sheet. Bake 10 minutes. Allow to cool before serving. Makes 36 cookies.

BROWNIES

PINK PEPPERMINT
FROSTED BROWNIES

1 (9 x 13-inch family size)	**brownie mix**
	ingredients listed on back of box
	red food coloring
1 container (16 ounces)	**vanilla frosting**
1 bag (10 ounces)	**Andes Peppermint Crunch**
	Baking Chips
3 tablespoons	**butter or margarine**
3 (1 ounce each)	**unsweetened or semisweet**
	chocolate squares

Prepare and bake brownies according to package directions in a greased 9 x 13-inch pan; cool. Stir drops of red food coloring into vanilla frosting until it reaches desired shade of pink. Frost brownies with pink frosting. Sprinkle peppermint chips over top.

In a small saucepan, melt butter and chocolate squares. Drizzle over top of brownies. Cool completely before cutting into squares. Makes 24 brownies.

ROCKY ROAD BROWNIES

I (9 x 13-inch family size) **brownie mix**
ingredients listed on back of box
I cup **salted peanuts**
2 cups **miniature marshmallows**
I cup **chocolate chips**

Preheat oven to 350 degrees.

Make batter according to package directions. Pour batter into a greased 9 x 13-inch pan. Bake 23–25 minutes. Remove brownies from oven. Sprinkle peanuts, marshmallows, and chocolate chips evenly over top. Bake an additional 3–5 minutes, or until marshmallows puff up. Makes 24 brownies.

DOCTORED-UP BROWNIES

1 (9 x 13-inch family size)	**brownie mix**
	ingredients listed on back of box
³/₄ cup	**M&M's, Reese's Pieces, mint chocolate pieces, peanut butter chips, butterscotch chips, chocolate chips, white chocolate chips, or nuts**
1 container (16 ounces)	**chocolate frosting**

Preheat oven to 350 degrees.

Make batter according to package directions. Stir in ³/₄ cup of any item chosen from above. Pour batter into a greased 9 x 13-inch pan. Bake 25 minutes, or until done. Allow brownies to cool. Spread frosting evenly over brownies. Sprinkle any extra candies over top. Makes 24 brownies.

VARIATION: Use a 9 x 9-inch size brownie mix with ¹/₂ cup candy, nuts, or baking chips.

COOKIE DOUGH BROWNIES

Bottom Layer:

1 (9 x 13-inch family size)	**brownie mix**
	ingredients listed on back of box
$1/2$ cup	**semisweet chocolate chips**

Filling:

$1/2$ cup	**butter or margarine,** softened
$1/2$ cup	**brown sugar**
$1/4$ cup	**sugar**
2 tablespoons	**milk**
1 teaspoon	**vanilla**
1 cup	**flour**

Topping:

1 tablespoon	**butter or margarine**
1 cup	**semisweet chocolate chips**

Preheat oven to 350 degrees.

Make batter according to package directions. Stir in chocolate chips. Pour batter into a greased 9 x 13-inch pan. Bake 25 minutes, or until done. Allow brownies to cool completely.

For the filling, mix butter, and sugars together in a bowl. Stir in milk and vanilla; mix in flour. Spread filling evenly over cooled brownies.

In a small saucepan, melt together butter and chocolate chips. Spread melted chocolate over filling. Nuts can be sprinkled on top, if desired. Cut into bars and refrigerate at least 2 hours; keep refrigerated. Makes 24 brownies.

EASY BROWNIES FROM SCRATCH

$^3/_4$ cup **butter or margarine,** melted
1$^1/_4$ cups **sugar**
1$^1/_2$ teaspoons **vanilla**
2 **eggs**
$^3/_4$ cup **flour**
$^1/_2$ cup **baking cocoa**
$^1/_4$ teaspoon **salt**
$^3/_4$ cup **chocolate chips**

Preheat oven to 350 degrees.

In a large bowl, combine butter, sugar, and vanilla; beat in eggs.

In a separate bowl, combine flour, cocoa, and salt. Slowly stir flour mixture into cream mixture. Pour batter into a greased 8 x 8-inch pan. Sprinkle chocolate chips over top and then bake 30–35 minutes; allow brownies to cool. Makes 10–12 brownies.

VARIATIONS: Use $^3/_4$ cup peanut butter chips in place of chocolate chips. Chopped Andes Mints or butterscotch chips can also be used in place of chocolate chips.

CARAMEL
CASHEW BROWNIES

1 (9 x 13-inch family size)	**brownie mix**
	ingredients listed on back of box
1 cup	**chopped cashews**
1 cup	**semisweet or milk chocolate chips**
25	**caramels,** unwrapped
1/8 cup	**milk**

Preheat oven to 350 degrees.

Make batter according to package directions. Stir in cashews and chocolate chips. Pour batter into a greased 9 x 13-inch pan. Bake 25 minutes, or until done; allow bars to cool 20–30 minutes.

In a saucepan, thoroughly melt caramels and milk together, stirring constantly. Pour caramel topping evenly over brownies. Cool completely and cut into bars. Makes 24 brownies.

CHOCOLATE MINT
LAYER BROWNIES

1 (9 x 13-inch family size)	**brownie mix**
	ingredients listed on back of box

Mint Layer:

2 cups	**powdered sugar**
1/2 cup	**butter or margarine,** softened
1 1/2 teaspoons	**mint extract**
3 to 4 drops	**green food coloring**

Chocolate Layer:

2 tablespoons	**butter or margarine**
1 cup	**semisweet or mint chocolate chips**
1 1/2 tablespoons	**milk**

Prepare and bake brownies according to package directions in a 9 x 13-inch pan. Allow brownies to cool completely.

For the mint layer, combine powdered sugar, butter, mint extract, and food coloring. Spread over cooled brownies.

For the chocolate layer, melt together butter, chocolate chips, and milk in a small saucepan. Spread over mint layer and allow to cool. Store leftovers in the refrigerator. Makes 24 brownies.

PEANUT BUTTER CUP BROWNIES

20	**miniature peanut butter cups**
1 (9 x 13-inch family size)	**brownie mix**
2	**eggs**
$1/2$ cup	**vegetable oil**
$1/4$ cup	**water**

Preheat oven to 350 degrees.

Unwrap and cut peanut butter cups in half.

In a bowl, mix together brownie mix, eggs, oil, and water. Stir in peanut butter cups. Pour batter into a greased 9 x 13-inch pan. Bake 28–30 minutes. Makes 24 brownies.

BARS

CHOCOLATE CARAMEL CANDY BARS

1	**chocolate cake mix**
$^1/_2$ cup	**butter or margarine,** melted
$^1/_4$ cup	**evaporated milk**
1 cup	**chocolate chips**
$^3/_4$ cup	**chopped nuts**
1 jar (12 ounces)	**caramel ice cream topping**

Preheat oven to 350 degrees.

In a bowl, mix together cake mix, butter, and milk until dough forms. Press three-fourths of the dough evenly into a greased 9 x 13-inch pan. Spread chocolate chips and nuts evenly over the dough. Pour caramel evenly over top. Break the rest of the dough into small pieces and drop evenly over the caramel. Bake 20–25 minutes. Cool 30 minutes and then cut into bars and refrigerate. Makes 24 bars.

CHOCOLATE PEANUT LAYER BARS

Bottom Layer:

1	**chocolate cake mix**
4 tablespoons	**butter or margarine,** melted
2	**eggs**
1/2 cup	**creamy peanut butter**

Top Layer:

1 can (14 ounces)	**sweetened condensed milk**
1 cup	**chocolate chips**
1 cup	**peanut butter chips**
1/2 cup	**chopped peanuts**

Preheat oven to 350 degrees.

In a bowl, mix together cake mix, butter, eggs, and peanut butter. Press dough evenly into a 9 x 13-inch pan that has been lightly sprayed with nonstick oil.

Pour sweetened condensed milk over the dough layer. Sprinkle chocolate chips, peanut butter chips, and peanuts evenly over top. Bake 20–25 minutes. Cool completely and cut into bars. Makes 24 bars.

PEANUT BUTTER CHIP COOKIE BARS

<table>
<tr><td>1</td><td>chocolate cake mix</td></tr>
<tr><td>2</td><td>eggs</td></tr>
<tr><td>$^1/_2$ cup</td><td>butter or margarine, melted</td></tr>
<tr><td>$^3/_4$ cup</td><td>chunky peanut butter</td></tr>
<tr><td>1 cup</td><td>peanut butter chips</td></tr>
</table>

Preheat oven to 350 degrees.

In a bowl, mix together cake mix, eggs, butter, and peanut butter until dough forms. Stir in peanut butter chips. Spread dough evenly into a greased 9 x 13-inch pan. Bake 23–25 minutes. Cut into bars and serve warm or at room temperature. Makes 24 bars.

VARIATION: For rich chocolate bars, use semisweet chocolate chips in place of peanut butter chips.

CHOCOLATE FALL HARVEST BARS

1 **devil's food cake mix**
2 **eggs**
$^1/_2$ cup **vegetable oil, butter, or margarine,** melted
$^1/_2$ cup **Skor toffee bits or crushed Butterfinger bars**
$^1/_2$ cup **chocolate chips**

Preheat oven to 350 degrees.

In a bowl, mix together cake mix, eggs, and oil or butter until dough forms. Stir in candy bits and chocolate chips. Spread dough evenly into a lightly greased 9 x 13-inch pan. Bake 18–20 minutes. Cut into bars and serve warm or at room temperature. Makes 24 bars.

CHOCOLATE PEANUT BUTTER FANTASY BARS

1	**chocolate cake mix**
1/2 cup	**butter or margarine,** melted
1	**egg**
1 1/2 cups	**coconut**
1 can (14 ounces)	**sweetened condensed milk**
2 cups	**semisweet chocolate chips**
1/2 cup	**creamy peanut butter**

Preheat oven to 350 degrees.

In a bowl, mix together cake mix, butter, and egg until smooth. Press dough evenly into a 9 x 13-inch glass pan. Sprinkle coconut over the top. Pour sweetened condensed milk evenly over coconut. Bake 20–25 minutes, or until edges are a light golden brown.

In a saucepan, melt together chocolate chips and peanut butter over low heat. Spread chocolate over hot coconut layer. Cool 30 minutes. Refrigerate and cut into bars. Makes 24 bars.

DECADENT SEMISWEET COOKIE BARS

27	**chocolate sandwich cookies**
4 tablespoons	**butter or margarine,** melted
2 cups	**semisweet chocolate chips,** divided
1 can (14 ounces)	**sweetened condensed milk**
1 teaspoon	**vanilla**

Preheat oven to 325 degrees.

Grind 21 of the cookies in a blender or food processor.

In a bowl, combine cookie crumbs and butter. Press crumb mixture evenly into a 9 x 13-inch pan.

In a saucepan, combine 1 cup chocolate chips, sweetened condensed milk, and vanilla over low heat, stirring until chocolate melts. Drizzle chocolate sauce evenly over crust. Sprinkle remaining chocolate chips over the top. Crumble remaining 6 cookies over top. Bake 20 minutes. Allow to cool. Refrigerate at least 2 hours and cut into bars. Makes 24 bars.

VARIATIONS: Use chocolate mint sandwich cookies, chocolate peanut butter–filled sandwich cookies, or any other variation of sandwich cookies.

CHOCOLATE LAYER BARS

1	**chocolate cake mix**
1/2 cup	**butter or margarine,** melted
1	**egg**
1 can (14 ounces)	**sweetened condensed milk**
1 cup	**coconut**
1 cup	**chocolate chips**
1 cup	**butterscotch chips**
1 bag (2 ounces)	**sliced almonds**

Preheat oven to 350 degrees.

In a bowl, mix together cake mix, butter, and egg. Press dough evenly into a 9 x 13-inch pan that has been lightly sprayed with nonstick oil. Pour sweetened condensed milk over the dough layer. Sprinkle coconut, chocolate chips, butterscotch chips, and nuts evenly over top. Bake 25 minutes. Cool completely and cut into bars. Make 24 bars.

CHOCOLATE CREAM CHEESE BARS

1	**chocolate cake mix**
2	**eggs**
1/2 cup	**butter or margarine,** softened
1 cup	**semisweet chocolate chips**
1 package (8 ounces)	**cream cheese,** softened
1/2 cup	**sugar**
1	**egg**

Preheat oven to 350 degrees.

In a bowl, mix together cake mix, eggs, and butter until smooth. Stir in chocolate chips. Press two-thirds of the dough evenly into a greased 8 x 8-inch pan.

In a separate bowl, mix together cream cheese, sugar, and egg until fairly smooth. Spread cream cheese mixture over the dough layer. Lay long, flat sections of remaining dough evenly over the top trying to cover as much as possible. Bake 35 minutes. Allow to cool completely. Refrigerate at least 2 hours before serving. Makes 12 bars.

PEANUT BUTTER CRUNCH BARS

1	**chocolate cake mix**
2	**eggs**
1/2 cup	**vegetable oil**
1/2 cup	**creamy or crunchy peanut butter**

Topping:

1 cup	**semisweet chocolate chips***
1/2 cup	**creamy peanut butter**
1 1/2 cups	**crispy rice cereal**

Preheat oven to 350 degrees.

In a bowl, mix together cake mix, eggs, and oil until dough forms. Stir in peanut butter. Spread dough evenly into a lightly greased 9 x 13-inch pan. Bake 18–20 minutes. Cool 20–25 minutes.

For the topping, melt chocolate chips and peanut butter together in a saucepan over low heat. Remove from heat. Fold cereal into melted chocolate sauce. Spread mixture evenly over bars. Cool completely and cut into bars. Makes 24 bars.

*For a sweeter chocolate taste, use milk chocolate chips instead of semisweet chocolate chips.

CHOCOLATE CHIP PUDDING BARS

1	**yellow or white cake mix**
2	**eggs**
$^1/_3$ cup	**vegetable oil**
1 cup	**chocolate chips**

Topping:

1 small box	**chocolate instant pudding mix**
$1^1/_2$ cups	**milk**

Preheat oven to 350 degrees.

In a bowl, mix together cake mix, eggs, and oil until dough forms. Stir in chocolate chips. Spread dough evenly into a lightly greased 9 x 13-inch pan. Bake 14–16 minutes. For a chewy consistency, pull the bars out when the edges are barely starting to turn a light golden brown. With the handles of a wooden spoon, immediately poke holes at 1-inch intervals.

In a separate bowl, beat together pudding mix and milk for 2 minutes with a wire whisk. Pour half the pudding over warm bars. Let the rest of the pudding chill and set up 5–10 minutes. Frost the bars with the remaining pudding. Refrigerate at least 1 hour before cutting and serving. Makes 24 bars.

WHITE CHOCOLATE ALMOND BARS

  1 **chocolate or yellow cake mix**
  2 **eggs**
  $^1/_2$ cup **butter or margarine,** softened
  1 cup **white chocolate chips**
  $^1/_2$ to $^3/_4$ cup **chopped almonds**

Preheat oven to 350 degrees.

In a bowl, mix together cake mix, eggs, and butter. Stir in white chocolate chips and chopped almonds; mixture will be stiff. Press dough into a greased 9 x 13-inch pan. Bake 15–18 minutes for a yellow cake mix and 20 minutes for a chocolate cake mix. Serve warm or at room temperature. Can be topped with favorite frosting, if desired. Makes 24 bars.

CHOCOLATE CHEESECAKE BARS

I	**chocolate cake mix**
I	**egg**
1/2 cup	**butter or margarine,** melted
I pound	**powdered sugar**
2	**eggs**
I package (8 ounces)	**cream cheese,** softened
I teaspoon	**vanilla**

Preheat oven to 350 degrees.

In a bowl, mix together cake mix and egg. Stir in butter. Spread dough evenly into a greased 9 x 13-inch pan.

In a separate bowl, mix together powdered sugar, eggs, cream cheese, and vanilla until smooth. Spread mixture over bottom layer. Bake 30–35 minutes. Makes 24 bars.

HELLO DOLLIES

$^1/_2$ cup **butter or margarine,** melted
2 cups **crushed graham crackers**
1 cup **chocolate chips**
1 cup **coconut**
$^2/_3$ cup **chopped nuts**
1 can (14 ounces) **sweetened condensed milk**

Preheat oven to 350 degrees.

Melt butter in a glass 9 x 13-inch pan in the oven. Sprinkle graham cracker crumbs over butter. Layer chocolate chips, coconut, and nuts over crust. Drizzle sweetened condensed milk over top. Bake 20 minutes. Makes 24 servings.

Cakes & Bundt Cakes

DOUBLE-CHOCOLATE ALMOND CAKE

I	**chocolate cake mix**
	ingredients listed on back of box
¹/₂ cup	**diced almonds**
³/₄ cup	**chocolate chips**

Topping:

I ¹/₂ cups	**milk**
I package (8 ounces)	**cream cheese,** softened
I small box	**chocolate instant pudding mix**
I container (8 ounces)	**frozen whipped topping,** thawed
	chocolate bar, shaved

Preheat oven to 350 degrees.

Make cake batter according to package directions. Stir almonds and chocolate chips into batter. Pour batter into a greased 9 x 13-inch pan. Bake 30–35 minutes, or until a toothpick inserted in the center comes out clean. Allow cake to cool to room temperature.

In a bowl, gradually beat milk into cream cheese. Stir in pudding mix. Spread over cooled cake. Spread whipped topping over top and garnish with chocolate shavings. Refrigerate until ready to serve. Makes 20–24 servings.

BANANA CHOCOLATE CHIP CAKE

2 cups	**flour**
1 teaspoon	**baking soda**
$^1/_4$ teaspoon	**salt**
$^1/_2$ cup	**butter or margarine,** softened
$^3/_4$ cup	**brown sugar**
2 cups	**mashed, ripe banana**
2	**eggs,** beaten
1 cup	**mini chocolate chips**
$^1/_2$ container (16 ounces)	**chocolate frosting**

Preheat oven to 350 degrees.

In a bowl, mix together flour, baking soda, and salt.

In a separate large bowl, mix together butter and brown sugar. Stir in banana and eggs into butter mixture. Gradually stir in one-third of the flour mixture at a time until flour is blended. Stir in chocolate chips. Pour batter into a greased 8 x 8-inch pan. Bake 32–38 minutes, or until a toothpick inserted in the center comes out clean. Allow cake to cool to room temperature. Frost with a thin layer of remaining chocolate frosting. Makes 12 servings.

BLACKBERRY CHOCOLATE CAKE

1	**chocolate cake mix**
3	**eggs**
1 can (21 ounces)	**blackberry pie filling**
1 cup	**chopped nuts**
1 cup	**chocolate chips**
$^1/_2$ cup	**brown sugar**

Preheat oven to 350 degrees.

In a bowl, combine cake mix, eggs, and pie filling. Spread mixture into a greased 9 x 13-inch pan. Sprinkle nuts, chocolate chips, and brown sugar over the top. Bake 30–35 minutes, or until a toothpick inserted in the center comes out clean. Makes 20–24 servings.

VARIATION: Strawberry or cherry pie filling can be used in place of blackberry pie filling.

CHOCOLATE PEANUT BUTTER CAKE

I	**chocolate cake mix**
	ingredients listed on back of box
1/2 cup	**chunky peanut butter**
I cup	**semisweet chocolate chips**

Frosting:

I container (16 ounces)	**chocolate frosting**
1/4 cup	**creamy peanut butter**
1/2 cup	**chopped peanuts** (optional)

Preheat oven to 350 degrees.

Make batter according to package directions. Mix in peanut butter with a hand mixer. With a spoon, stir in chocolate chips. Pour batter into a greased 9 x 13-inch pan. Bake 25–30 minutes, or until a toothpick inserted in the center comes out clean. Allow cake to cool completely.

In a bowl, mix frosting and peanut butter together. Spread over top of cooled cake. Sprinkle with chopped peanuts, if desired. Makes 20–24 servings.

ENTERTAINING DELIGHT CAKE

I	**devil's food cake mix**
	ingredients listed on back of box
I cup	**semisweet chocolate chips**
I large box	**chocolate instant pudding mix**
I container (8 ounces)	**frozen whipped topping,** thawed
	chocolate bar, shaved

Preheat oven to 350 degrees.

Mix batter according to package directions with a hand mixer for 2 minutes. Stir in chocolate chips. Pour the batter into a greased 9 x 13-inch pan. Bake for the amount of time instructed on the back of the box. Allow cake to cool.

While cake is cooling, make pudding according to package directions. Allow pudding to set up in the refrigerator. Cut the cake into long skinny pieces, about $1 \frac{1}{2}$ x 3 inches. Place one slice of cake on a small plate. Place a large scoop of pudding over the cake. Place another slice of cake over the top of pudding. Scoop some more pudding on cake. Top with whipped topping. Using a vegetable peeler, shave chocolate from chocolate bar over the whipped topping. Makes 12 servings.

BUTTERFINGER SHEET CAKE

1 1/4 cups **butter or margarine,** divided
1/2 cup **baking cocoa,** divided
1 cup **water**
2 cups **flour**
1 1/2 cups **brown sugar**
1 teaspoon **baking soda**
1/2 teaspoon **salt**
1 can (14 ounces) **sweetened condensed milk,** divided
2 **eggs**
1 teaspoon **vanilla**
1 cup **powdered sugar**
6 **fun-size Butterfinger candy bars**

Preheat oven to 350 degrees.

In a small saucepan pan, melt 1 cup butter. Stir in 1/4 cup cocoa and water; bring to a boil. Remove from heat.

In a large bowl, mix together flour, brown sugar, baking soda, and salt. Beat into batter the cocoa mixture, 1/3 cup sweetened condensed milk, eggs, and vanilla until smooth. Pour batter into a greased baking sheet with sides. Bake 15 to 20 minutes.

Make frosting by combining 1/4 cup melted butter, remaining cocoa, and remaining sweetened condensed milk in a bowl; stir in powdered sugar and then spread over warm cake. Sprinkle crushed Butterfinger over top. Makes 24–28 servings.

Rich VARIATION: Stir 1/2 cup mini chocolate chips into batter for an extra dose of chocolate.

Coconut VARIATION: Sprinkle 1 cup coconut over cake in place of Butterfinger.

MOIST CHOCOLATE
MAYONNAISE CAKE

1	**chocolate cake mix**
4	**eggs**
1 cup	**mayonnaise**
1 cup	**water**
2 cups	**miniature marshmallows**
1 cup	**semisweet or milk chocolate chips**
1 cup	**chopped nuts**
	powdered sugar or chocolate syrup

Preheat oven to 350 degrees.

In a bowl, mix together cake mix, eggs, mayonnaise, and water with a hand mixer for 2 minutes. Stir in marshmallows, chocolate chips, and nuts. Pour batter into a greased 10-inch fluted-tube pan. Bake 45–50 minutes, or until cake springs back when touched. Remove from oven and let sit 5 minutes.

While still hot, invert onto a serving platter; cool completely. Sprinkle powdered sugar or drizzle chocolate syrup over the top to decorate. Makes 16 servings.

CHOCOLATE PEANUT BUTTER CANDY CAKE

1	**chocolate cake mix**
	ingredients listed on back of box
1 1/2 cups	**Reese's Pieces, peanut M&M's, or**
	peanut butter M&M's
2 teaspoons	**flour**

Frosting:
1 container (16 ounces)	**chocolate frosting**
1/4 cup	**creamy peanut butter**

Preheat oven to 350 degrees.

Make batter according to package directions.

In a sandwich bag, shake candy with flour. With a spoon, stir candy into cake batter. Then pour the batter into a greased 9 x 13-inch pan. Bake 30–40 minutes. Allow cake to cool completely.

In a bowl, mix frosting and peanut butter together. Frost cake and serve. For a fun border, place extra candies around the outer edge. Makes 20–24 servings.

CHERRY-CHOCOLATE BUNDT CAKE

1	**chocolate cake mix**
3	**eggs**
1 can (21 ounces)	**cherry pie filling**
1 container (16 ounces)	**chocolate frosting** or 1 can
	(21 ounces) **cherry pie filling**

Preheat oven to 350 degrees.

In a bowl, mix together cake mix and eggs. Stir in 1 can pie filling until cake mix is completely dissolved into batter. Pour batter into a greased bundt pan. Bake 40–50 minutes, or until a toothpick inserted in the center comes out clean.

While still hot, invert the cake onto a platter. When cool, frost with chocolate frosting or spread pie filling over top. Makes 16 servings.

SWEET-GLAZED
CHOCOLATE BUNDT CAKE

4	**eggs**
³/₄ cup	**sour cream**
¹/₂ cup	**water**
¹/₂ cup	**oil**
1	**white cake mix**
1 small box	**chocolate instant pudding mix**
1 cup	**chocolate chips**

Chocolate Glaze:

³/₄ cup	**semisweet chocolate chips**
1 tablespoon	**corn syrup**
3 tablespoons	**butter or margarine**
¹/₄ teaspoon	**vanilla**

Preheat oven to 350 degrees.

In a large bowl, beat together eggs, sour cream, water, and oil until thoroughly mixed. Stir in cake mix and pudding mix. Fold in chocolate chips. Pour batter into a greased-and-floured bundt pan. Bake 45–50 minutes, or until a toothpick inserted in the center comes out clean. While still hot, invert the cake onto a platter; allow cake to cool.

In a heavy saucepan, combine chocolate chips, corn syrup, and butter. Stir over low heat until chocolate is melted; stir in vanilla. Spread warm glaze over top of cake, allowing glaze to drizzle down the sides. Makes 16 servings.

VARIATION: Use a chocolate cake mix and white chocolate pudding in place of the white cake mix and chocolate pudding.

ICE CREAM CAKES & SANDWICHES

COLORFUL ICE CREAM SANDWICHES

1	**chocolate or white cake mix**
$^1/_2$ cup	**oil, butter, or margarine,** melted
2	**eggs**
1 to 1$^1/_2$ cups	**plain M&M's**
$^1/_2$ gallon	**vanilla or chocolate ice cream**

Preheat oven to 350 degrees.

In a large bowl, mix together cake mix, oil, and eggs. The dough will be stiff. Mix in M&M's. Using a cookie scoop, drop dough by teaspoonfuls onto a baking sheet. Bake 8–12 minutes. Remove cookies from the oven and allow to set up on hot baking sheet for 3 minutes. Remove from pan and place on nonstick cooling rack to cool. Once completely cooled, place a scoopful of ice cream between two cookies. Wrap the sandwiches in plastic wrap. Store cookies in an airtight container in the freezer. Makes 16–18 ice cream sandwiches.

GRASSHOPPER ICE CREAM SANDWICHES

1	**chocolate cake mix**
$^1/_2$ cup	**butter or margarine,** softened
2	**eggs**
1 cup	**green mint chips**
$^1/_2$ gallon	**mint chocolate chip ice cream**

Preheat oven to 350 degrees.

In a large bowl, mix together cake mix, butter, and eggs. The dough will be stiff. Mix in mint chips. Using a cookie scoop, drop dough by teaspoonfuls onto a baking sheet. Bake 8–12 minutes. Remove cookies from oven and allow to set up on hot baking sheet for 2–3 minutes. Remove from pan and place on nonstick cooling rack to cool. Once completely cooled, place a scoopful of ice cream between two cookies. Wrap the sandwiches in plastic wrap. Store cookies in an airtight container in the freezer. Makes 16–18 ice cream sandwiches.

NUTTY CHOCOLATE CHIP ICE CREAM SANDWICHES

1	**white cake mix**
$1/2$ cup	**butter or margarine,** softened
2	**eggs**
1 cup	**semisweet or milk chocolate chips**
$1/2$ cup	**chopped nuts**
$1/2$ gallon	**chocolate ice cream**

Preheat oven to 350 degrees.

In a large bowl, mix together cake mix, butter, and eggs. The dough will be stiff. Mix in chocolate chips and nuts. Using a cookie scoop, drop dough by teaspoonfuls onto a baking sheet. Bake 8–12 minutes. Remove cookies from oven and allow to set up on hot baking sheet for 2–3 minutes. Remove from pan and place on nonstick cooling rack to cool. Once completely cooled, place a scoopful of ice cream between two cookies. Wrap the sandwiches in plastic wrap. Store cookies in an airtight container in the freezer. Makes 16–18 ice cream sandwiches.

BROWNIE ICE CREAM CAKE

1	**chocolate cake mix**
1/2 cup	**butter or margarine,** melted
1	**egg**
1/2 cup	**chopped or grated nuts**
1 1/2 boxes (1/2 gallon each)	**vanilla or fudge ripple ice cream,** softened
1 jar (11.75 ounces)	**fudge ice cream topping**
	chopped nuts or chocolate chips, optional

Preheat oven to 350 degrees.

In a bowl, mix together cake mix, butter, and egg. Stir in nuts. Press dough evenly into a lightly greased 9 x 13-inch pan. Bake 10–12 minutes, or until a toothpick inserted in the center comes out clean. With a fork, remove the air pockets by pushing down evenly over the entire hot crust. Allow crust to cool completely.

Spread softened ice cream evenly over crust. Spread ice cream topping evenly over ice cream. Sprinkle nuts or chocolate chips over top, if desired. Cover and freeze at least 4 hours before serving. Makes 20 servings.

INSTANT ICE CREAM
SANDWICH CAKE

I jar (16 ounces)	**chocolate syrup**
³/₄ cup	**peanut butter**
19	**ice cream sandwiches**
I container (12 ounces)	**frozen whipped topping,** thawed
I¹/₄ cups	**chopped salted peanuts,** divided

Heat chocolate syrup for 2 minutes in the microwave. Stir peanut
butter into hot syrup; allow to cool. Line the bottom of a 9 x 13-inch
glass pan with a layer of ice cream sandwiches. Spread half the chocolate mixture over sandwiches. Cover with half the whipped topping.
Sprinkle ¹/₂ cup peanuts over top. Repeat with another layer of ice
cream sandwiches, remaining chocolate mixture, remaining whipped
topping, and remaining nuts. Freeze I hour or more until ready to
serve. Makes 20 servings.

COOKIE DOUGH ICE CREAM CAKE

1	**chocolate, yellow, or white cake mix**
1/2 cup	**butter or margarine,** melted
1	**egg**
1 1/2 cups	**mini chocolate chips,** divided
1 1/2 boxes (1/2 gallon each)	**chocolate chip cookie dough ice cream,** softened
1 jar (11.75 ounces)	**fudge or caramel ice cream topping**

Preheat oven to 350 degrees.

In a bowl, mix together cake mix, butter, and egg. Stir in 1 cup chocolate chips. Press dough evenly into a lightly greased 9 x 13-inch pan. Bake 10–12 minutes. Crust will still be doughy. With a fork, remove the air pockets by pushing down evenly over the entire hot crust; allow crust to cool completely.

Open boxes so they lay flat and cut softened ice cream into equal-size slices. Spread half the ice cream evenly over crust. Spread fudge or caramel over the first layer of ice cream. Spread remaining ice cream slices over top. Sprinkle remaining chocolate chips over top. Cover and freeze at least 4 hours before serving. Makes 20 servings.

COOKIES-AND-CREAM ICE CREAM CAKE

1	**chocolate or white cake mix**
1/2 cup	**butter or margarine,** melted
1	**egg**
1 1/2 boxes (1/2 gallon each)	**cookies and cream ice cream,** softened
1 jar (11.75 ounces)	**fudge ice cream topping**
2 cups	**chopped chocolate sandwich cookies,** divided

Preheat oven to 350 degrees.

In a bowl, mix together cake mix, butter, and egg. Press dough evenly into a lightly greased 9 x 13-inch pan. Bake 10–12 minutes. Crust will still be doughy. With a fork, remove the air pockets by pushing down evenly over the entire hot crust; allow crust to cool completely.

Open boxes so they lay flat and cut softened ice cream into equal-size slices. Spread half the ice cream evenly over crust. Soften fudge in microwave if needed and then drizzle evenly over ice cream. Sprinkle 1 cup chopped cookies over fudge. Spread remaining ice cream sliced over cookie layer. Sprinkle remaining chopped cookies over top. Cover and freeze at least 4 hours before serving. Makes 20 servings.

MINT CHOCOLATE CHIP ICE CREAM CAKE

1	**chocolate cake mix**
1/2 cup	**butter or margarine,** melted
1	**egg**
1 1/2 to 2 boxes (1/2 gallon each)	**mint chocolate chip ice cream,** softened
1 jar (11.75 ounces)	**fudge ice cream topping**

Preheat oven to 350 degrees.

In a bowl, mix together cake mix, butter, and egg. Press dough evenly into a lightly greased 9 x 13-inch pan. Bake 10–12 minutes. Crust will still be doughy. With a fork, remove the air pockets by pushing down evenly over the entire hot crust; allow crust to cool completely.

Open boxes so they lay flat and cut softened ice cream into equal-size slices. Spread ice cream evenly over crust. Drizzle ice cream topping evenly over ice cream. Cover and freeze at least 4 hours before serving. Makes 20 servings.

PEANUT BUTTER CHOCOLATE ICE CREAM CAKE

I	**chocolate cake mix**
¹/₂ cup	**butter or margarine,** melted
I	**egg**
³/₄ cup	**peanut butter chips**
I ¹/₂ to 2 boxes (¹/₂ gallon each)	**chocolate or peanut butter chocolate ice cream**
²/₃ cup	**peanut butter,** softened
I cup	**corn syrup**
³/₄ cup	**chopped peanuts,** optional

Preheat oven to 350 degrees.

In a bowl, mix together cake mix, butter, and egg. Stir in peanut butter chips. Press dough evenly into a lightly greased 9 x 13-inch pan. Bake 10–12 minutes. Crust will still be doughy. With a fork, remove the air pockets by pushing down evenly over the entire hot crust; allow crust to cool completely.

Open boxes so they lay flat and cut softened ice cream into equal-size slices. Spread ice cream evenly over crust. Soften peanut butter in microwave for 10–30 seconds on high. Stir in corn syrup. Pour topping over the ice cream. Sprinkle chopped peanuts over top if desired. Cover and freeze at least 4 hours before serving. Makes 20 servings.

ROCKY ROAD ICE CREAM CAKE

1	**chocolate or white cake mix**
1/2 cup	**butter or margarine**
1	**egg**
1 1/2 to 2 boxes (1/2 gallon each)	**rocky road ice cream,** softened
1 jar (11.75 ounces)	**marshmallow or fudge ice cream topping**
1/2 cup	**chopped nuts**
1/2 cup	**mini chocolate chips**
3/4 cup	**miniature marshmallows**

Preheat oven to 350 degrees.

In a bowl, mix together cake mix, butter, and egg. Press dough evenly into a lightly greased 9 x 13-inch pan. Bake 10–12 minutes. Crust will still be doughy. With a fork, remove the air pockets by pushing down evenly over the entire hot crust; allow crust to cool completely.

Open boxes so they lay flat and cut softened ice cream into equal-size slices. Spread ice cream evenly over crust. Microwave ice cream topping 15–20 seconds, stir, and spread evenly over ice cream. Sprinkle nuts, chocolate chips, and marshmallows over top. Cover and freeze at least 4 hours or overnight. Makes 20 servings.

VARIATION: Vanilla or chocolate ice cream can be substituted for rocky road ice cream.

Cheesecakes, Dessert Pizzas, & Pies

CANDY BAR CHEESECAKE

1 1/2 cups	**crushed chocolate sandwich cookies**
4 tablespoons	**butter or margarine,** melted
3 packages (8 ounces each)	**cream cheese,** softened
3/4 cup	**sugar**
1 1/2 teaspoons	**vanilla**
3	**eggs**
4	**Snickers candy bars,** chilled and thinly sliced
1 bag (11.5 ounces)	**chocolate chips**
1 tablespoon	**shortening**

Preheat oven to 300 degrees.

In a small bowl, combine cookie crumbs and butter and press over bottom and up the sides of a 9-inch springform pan.

In a large bowl, beat together cream cheese, sugar, and vanilla. Beat in eggs one at a time until smooth; fold in 3 sliced candy bars. Pour cream cheese mixture over crust. Bake 1 hour. Turn off oven without opening the door and leave cheesecake in oven 1 hour more.

Melt chocolate chips and shortening together in the microwave 45–60 seconds; stir until smooth. Spread chocolate over cheesecake. Refrigerate 6 hours or overnight. Arrange remaining candy bar slices over top. Makes 10–12 servings.

CHOCOLATE CHIP CHEESECAKE

1 1/2 cups	**chocolate graham cracker crumbs**
1/4 cup	**sugar**
1/3 cup	**butter or margarine,** melted
3 packages (8 ounces each)	**cream cheese,** softened
2 teaspoons	**vanilla**
3	**eggs**
1 can (14 ounces)	**sweetened condensed milk**
1 1/2 cups	**mini semisweet chocolate chips,** divided
1 teaspoon	**flour**

Preheat oven to 300 degrees.

In a small bowl, combine graham cracker crumbs, sugar, and butter. Press over bottom and up the sides of a 9-inch springform pan.

In a large bowl, beat together cream cheese and vanilla. Beat in eggs one at a time until smooth. Slowly mix in sweetened condensed milk. Toss 1/2 cup mini chocolate chips with flour. Fold coated chocolate chips into cream cheese mixture. Pour mixture into crust. Bake 1 hour. Turn off oven without opening the door and leave cheesecake in oven 1 hour more. Remove from oven and sprinkle 1 cup mini chocolate chips over top. Refrigerate 6–8 hours or overnight. Makes 10–12 servings.

FUDGE TRUFFLE CHEESECAKE

1 1/2 cups	**vanilla wafer crumbs**
1/2 cup	**powdered sugar**
1/3 cup	**baking cocoa**
1/2 cup	**butter or margarine,** melted
3 packages (8 ounces each)	**cream cheese,** softened
1 can (14 ounces)	**sweetened condensed milk**
4	**eggs**
1 1/2 teaspoons	**vanilla**
1 bag (11.5 ounces)	**semisweet chocolate chips**

Preheat oven to 300 degrees.

In a bowl, combine wafer crumbs, powdered sugar, cocoa, and butter. Press mixture into the bottom of a greased 9-inch springform pan.

In a large bowl, beat cream cheese, sweetened condensed milk, eggs, and vanilla together until smooth.

In a heavy 1 1/2-quart saucepan, melt chocolate chips, stirring constantly. Stir melted chocolate into cream cheese mixture. Pour chocolate cream cheese mixture over crust. Bake 1 hour. Turn off oven without opening the door and leave cheesecake in oven 1 hour more. Refrigerate 3–4 hours or overnight. Makes 10–12 servings.

CHOCOLATE STRAWBERRY CHEESECAKE BARS

I	**chocolate cake mix**
$^1/_2$ cup	**butter or margarine,** melted
I	**egg**
I jar (18 ounces)	**seedless strawberry jam,** divided
2 packages (8 ounces each)	**cream cheese,** softened
$^3/_4$ cup	**sugar**
$^1/_2$ teaspoon	**vanilla**
3	**eggs**
	chocolate syrup

Preheat oven to 350 degrees.

In a bowl, mix together cake mix, butter, and egg. Spread dough evenly into a greased 9 x 13-inch pan. Stir jam until smooth then spread I cup jam evenly over crust.

In a separate bowl, mix together cream cheese, sugar, and vanilla. Beat in eggs one at a time. Pour over the jam layer. Bake 30 minutes, or until cheesecake is set and firm in the center; remove from oven and allow to cool.

In a saucepan, warm I cup jam over medium heat. Drizzle jam evenly over cooled cheesecake. Refrigerate 2–3 hours or overnight. To decorate, drizzle chocolate syrup over top before cutting into bars and serving. Makes 20–24 servings.

COCONUT ALMOND PIZZA

1	**chocolate cake mix**
2	**eggs**
1/2 cup	**butter or margarine,** melted
1 can (14 ounces)	**sweetened condensed milk**
3/4 cup	**sliced almonds**
1 cup	**shredded coconut**
1 cup	**semisweet chocolate chips**
2 1/2 tablespoons	**milk**

Preheat oven to 350 degrees.

In a bowl, mix together cake mix, eggs, and butter until cake mix is completely worked into the dough. Spread dough thinly to cover a jellyroll pan or baking sheet. Bake 12 minutes, or until crust begins to crack and appears to be done; cool completely. Pour sweetened condensed milk evenly over crust. Sprinkle almonds and coconut over top.

In a saucepan, melt chocolate chips and milk together until smooth. Drizzle chocolate over pizza. Makes 24–28 servings.

BANANA SPLIT PIZZA

1	**chocolate cake mix**
2	**eggs**
$1/2$ cup	**vegetable oil, butter, or margarine,** melted
$1/4$ cup	**powdered sugar**
1 package (8 ounces)	**cream cheese,** softened
1 container (8 ounces)	**frozen whipped topping,** thawed
1 can (8 ounces)	**pineapple chunks,** drained
2	**bananas,** thinly sliced
$3/4$ cup	**chopped peanuts or almonds**
$1\,1/2$ cups	**sliced strawberries**
	chocolate syrup, optional

Preheat oven to 350 degrees.

In a bowl, mix together cake mix, eggs, and oil until cake mix is completely worked into the dough. Spread the dough thinly to cover a jelly-roll pan or baking sheet. Bake 12 minutes, or until crust begins to crack and appears to be done; cool completely.

In a separate bowl, mix together powdered sugar, cream cheese, and whipped topping. Spread over crust. Evenly top with fruit and nuts. Drizzle chocolate syrup over the top to decorate, if desired. Serve immediately. Makes 24–28 servings.

CHOCOLATE CHIP COOKIE PIZZA

I	**yellow or white cake mix**
$^1/_2$ cup	**butter or margarine,** melted
2	**eggs**
I cup	**semisweet or milk chocolate chips**
I $^1/_2$ cups	**milk**
I small box	**chocolate instant pudding mix**
$^1/_2$ cup	**plain yogurt**
$^1/_3$ cup	**peanut butter**
	sliced bananas, shredded coconut, chocolate chips, peanuts, miniature marshmallows, or chopped candy bars

Preheat oven to 350 degrees.

In a bowl, mix together cake mix, butter, and eggs until cake mix is completely worked into the dough; stir in chocolate chips. Spread the dough thinly to cover a jellyroll pan or baking sheet. Bake 10–12 minutes, or until done; allow to cool completely.

In a separate bowl, mix together milk, pudding mix, yogurt, and peanut butter until smooth and thick. Chill 5–10 minutes, or until pudding mixture sets; spread over crust. Sprinkle your favorite toppings over top. Refrigerate before and after serving. Makes 24–28 servings.

CANDY BAR PUDDING PIE

2 **Snickers bars,** cut into $^1/_2$-inch pieces
I (6-ounce) **chocolate ready-made crumb crust**
I $^3/_4$ cups **milk**
I small box **chocolate instant pudding mix**

Sprinkle three-fourths of the candy bar pieces into piecrust.

In a bowl, whisk together milk and pudding mix until pudding begins to thicken. Spread pudding into piecrust. Refrigerate pie at least I hour, or until ready to serve. Sprinkle remaining candy bar pieces over top. Makes 6–8 servings.

VARIATIONS: Try using peanut butter cups, Baby Ruth candy bars, or other favorite candy bars in place of Snickers.

CHOCOLATE MOUSSE PIE

I package (3 ounces)	**cream cheese,** softened
$1/2$ cup	**sugar**
I teaspoon	**vanilla**
$1/3$ cup	**baking cocoa**
$1/3$ cup	**milk**
I container (8 ounces)	**frozen whipped topping,** thawed
I (6-ounce)	**ready-made chocolate crumb crust**

In a large bowl, mix together cream cheese, sugar, and vanilla until smooth; stir in cocoa and milk. Fold in whipped topping and then spoon filling into piecrust. Freeze 6 hours or overnight. Garnish with mini chocolate chips, if desired. Makes 6–8 servings.

COOKIES-AND-CREAM ICE CREAM PIE

¹/₂ gallon	**cookies and cream ice cream,** softened
1 (6-ounce)	**ready-made chocolate crumb crust**
5 to 7	**chocolate sandwich cookies,** crumbled

Spoon and spread ice cream into piecrust. Freeze 1 hour or more before serving. Sprinkle crumbled cookies over top. Garnish with whipped topping, if desired. Makes 6–8 servings.

VARIATIONS: Use cookie dough ice cream and sprinkle ¹/₂ cup mini chocolate chips over top. Use any type of candy bar ice cream and sprinkle 1 chopped candy bar over top.

FAMILY
FAVORITES

HOT CHOCOLATE

¹/4 cup **cocoa**
¹/2 cup **sugar**
¹/3 cup **water**
dash of **salt**
8 cups **milk**
I teaspoon **vanilla**

In a 3-quart saucepan, combine cocoa, sugar, water, and salt; bring to a boil. Stir in milk and cook over medium heat until hot; stir in vanilla. Pour into 8 glasses. Garnish with whipped topping or mini marshmallows, if desired. Makes 8 servings.

VARIATIONS: Add I teaspoon amaretto flavoring or mint extract instead of vanilla.

COOKIES-AND-CREAM MILKSHAKE

¹/₂ box (¹/₂ gallon)	**vanilla ice cream**
8	**double-stuffed chocolate sandwich cookies,** broken
1 to 1¹/₂ cups	**milk**

Combine all ingredients in the blender and blend for 30–60 seconds. For thicker shakes, use 1 cup milk. For thinner shakes, use 1¹/₂ cups milk. Garnish each shake with extra crumbled sandwich cookies. Makes 4 shakes.

NO-BAKE PEANUT BUTTER OATMEAL SQUARES

2 cups **sugar**
$^1/_4$ cup **unsweetened cocoa**
$^1/_2$ cup **milk**
$^1/_2$ cup **butter or margarine**
I teaspoon **vanilla**
I pinch **salt**
$^1/_2$ cup **chunky peanut butter**
3$^1/_4$ cups **quick oats**

In a 3-quart heavy saucepan, combine sugar, cocoa, milk, and butter.
Bring to a boil, stirring occasionally; boil I–I$^1/_2$ minutes. Remove
from heat and stir in vanilla, salt, and peanut butter; fold in oats until
covered. Spoon mixture into a buttered 9 x 13-inch pan. Chill 30 minutes and then cut into squares. Store leftovers in an airtight container.
Makes 24 squares.

CHOCOLATE CREAM CHEESE CUPCAKES

I	**devil's food or German chocolate cake mix**
	ingredients listed on back of box
I package (8 ounces)	**cream cheese,** softened
I	**egg**
^{1}/3 cup	**sugar**
I cup	**semisweet or milk chocolate chips**
I container (16 ounces)	**chocolate or white frosting**

Preheat oven to 350 degrees.

Mix cake batter according to package directions until smooth. Place paper cupcake liners in muffin pan. Fill muffin cups half full with batter.

In a separate bowl, combine cream cheese, egg, and sugar until smooth. Stir in chocolate chips. Place a tablespoon of cream filling in the center of each cupcake. Bake 18–22 minutes. Remove cupcakes from pan and cool completely. Top with frosting. Makes at least 24 cupcakes.

VARIATION: Butterscotch or peanut butter chips can be substituted for chocolate chips.

CHOCOLATE PEANUT BUTTER SURPRISE CUPCAKES

I	**chocolate cake mix**
	ingredients listed on back of box
I cup	**peanut butter chips**
24	**bite-size Snickers or miniature**
	peanut butter cups, unwrapped
I container (16 ounces)	**chocolate frosting**

Preheat oven to 350 degrees.

Mix cake batter according to package directions until smooth. With a spoon, fold in the peanut butter chips. Fill muffin cups one-third full. Bake 7–8 minutes. Place candy in center of each cupcake. Top candy with cake batter to fill muffin cups three-fourths full. Bake an additional 15–18 minutes, or until the top springs back when touched. Remove from pan and allow to cool completely. Top cupcakes with frosting. Makes 24 cupcakes.

CHOCOLATE-COVERED CEREAL SQUARES

1 cup	**sugar**
1/2 cup	**corn syrup**
1 teaspoon	**vanilla**
3/4 cup	**creamy peanut butter**
4 1/2 cups	**corn flakes**
1 bag (11.5 ounces)	**chocolate chips**
2 tablespoons	**milk**

In a nonstick 3- to 4-quart pan, bring sugar and corn syrup to a boil. Boil until sugar dissolves. Stir in vanilla and peanut butter until smooth; remove from heat. Fold in corn flakes until evenly coated. Spread into a greased 9 x 13-inch pan.

In a saucepan, melt chocolate chips and milk together, stirring constantly until smooth. Spread melted chocolate over cereal layer; cut into bars. Serve chilled or at room temperature. Makes 24 squares.

BUTTERSCOTCH CHOCOLATE CRISPY SQUARES

1 cup	**butterscotch chips**
1/2 cup	**peanut butter**
4 cups	**crispy rice cereal**
1 cup	**chocolate chips**
1 tablespoon	**water**
1/2 cup	**powdered sugar**
2 tablespoons	**butter or margarine**

In a saucepan, melt butterscotch chips and peanut butter together. Stir in cereal. Press half the cereal mixture into a 9 x 9-inch pan.

In a saucepan, combine chocolate chips, water, powdered sugar, and butter over low heat. Stir occasionally until chocolate is melted. Pour chocolate mixture evenly over cereal layer. Press the remaining cereal mixture on top. Chill 1 hour or until set. Allow bars to come to room temperature before cutting them to serve. Makes 16 squares.

CHOCOLATE LUSH

1 cup	**butter or margarine,** softened
1 cup	**flour**
$^1/_2$ cup	**chopped nuts,** optional
1 package (8 ounces)	**cream cheese,** softened
1 cup	**powdered sugar**
1 container (12 ounces)	**frozen whipped topping,** thawed and divided
2 small boxes	**chocolate instant pudding mix**
3 cups	**milk**

Preheat oven to 350 degrees.

Combine butter, flour, and nuts, if desired, with pastry blender until crumbly. Press mixture into a glass 9 x 13-inch pan. Bake 10 minutes; cool completely.

In a bowl, mix together cream cheese and powdered sugar. Fold in 1 cup whipped topping. Spread cream cheese mixture over cooled crust. Mix together pudding mixes and milk until pudding starts to thicken. Pour pudding over cream cheese layer. Spread remaining whipped topping over top. Refrigerate at least 1 hour, or until ready to serve. Makes 20–24 servings.

GRAHAM CRACKER CHOCOLATE SQUARES

2 cups	**graham cracker crumbs**
2 cups	**coconut**
$^1/_4$ cup	**butter or margarine,** melted
1 can (14 ounces)	**sweetened condensed milk**
1 cup	**chocolate chips**

Preheat oven to 400 degrees.

In a large bowl, combine all ingredients. Spread mixture into a greased 8 x 8-inch pan. Bake 15 minutes and cool 5 minutes; cut into squares and serve warm. Makes 16 squares.

PEANUT BUTTER CHOCOLATE CRISPY TREATS

I cup	**creamy peanut butter**
4 tablespoons	**butter or margarine**
I bag (16 ounces)	**miniature marshmallows**
7 cups	**crispy rice cereal**
I bag (11.5 ounces)	**milk chocolate chips**
2 tablespoons	**milk**

In a 3- to 4-quart pan, melt peanut butter and butter together until smooth. Stir marshmallows into peanut butter mixture until melted. Fold in cereal until evenly coated. Press cereal mixture into a lightly buttered 9 x 13-inch pan.

In a small heavy saucepan, melt chocolate chips and milk together until smooth. Spread chocolate evenly over cereal layer. Chill in refrigerator 1–2 hours, or until chocolate is hard. Makes 24 bars.

CHOCOLATE CHIP BANANA BREAD

$^1/_2$ cup	**butter or margarine,** softened
$^3/_4$ cup	**brown sugar**
2	**eggs,** beaten
2 cups	**mashed overripe bananas**
1 $^1/_2$ teaspoons	**pumpkin pie spice**
2 cups	**flour**
1 teaspoon	**baking soda**
$^1/_4$ teaspoon	**salt**
1 cup	**chocolate chips**

Preheat oven to 350 degrees.

In a large bowl, combine butter and brown sugar. Stir in eggs, bananas, and spice.

In a separate bowl, combine flour, baking soda, and salt. Slowly stir flour mixture into banana mixture until just moistened; fold in chocolate chips. Pour batter into a greased 9 x 5-inch loaf pan. Bake 50–55 minutes, or until bread springs back when touched in center. Allow bread to cool in pan 10 minutes before inverting onto a serving platter or wire rack. Makes 10–12 servings.

PEANUT BUTTER CHOCOLATE SQUARES

2^1/$_2$ cups **graham cracker crumbs***
1 cup **creamy peanut butter**
2^3/$_4$ cups **powdered sugar**
1 cup **butter or margarine,** melted
1 cup **semisweet chocolate chips**
1 cup **milk chocolate chips**

In a bowl, combine graham cracker crumbs, peanut butter, powdered sugar, and butter. Press mixture into a glass 9 x 13-inch pan.

Over a double boiler or in the microwave, melt chocolate chips. Spread melted chocolate over peanut butter layer. Allow chocolate to harden before cutting into bars. (Speed up the hardening process by placing bars in the refrigerator or freezer. Just make sure to allow bars to return to room temperature before cutting or the chocolate top will crack.) Makes 30–40 squares.

*15 whole graham crackers broken and crumbled equals approximately 2^1/$_2$ cups.

OATMEAL CARAMELITOS

2 cups	**flour**
1 1/2 cups	**brown sugar**
1/2 teaspoon	**salt**
2 cups	**oats**
1 teaspoon	**baking powder**
1 1/2 cups	**butter or margarine,** softened
1 package (11.5 ounces)	**milk chocolate chips**
1 cup	**chopped nuts**
2 jars (12.25 ounces each)	**caramel ice cream topping**

Preheat oven to 350 degrees.

In a bowl, combine flour, brown sugar, salt, oats, and baking powder.
Using a fork, cut butter into flour mixture until crumbly. Press half the
mixture into a jelly roll pan or baking sheet. Bake 10 minutes. Remove
from oven and immediately sprinkle chocolate chips over top. Allow
chocolate to melt and spread evenly over top. Sprinkle nuts over
chocolate layer. Pour caramel over chocolate and nuts. Sprinkle remaining oat crumbs over caramel. Bake 15–20 minutes; cool completely
before serving. Makes 28–32 bars.

CHOCOLATE PUDDING-FILLED DONUTS

2½ tablespoons	**active dry yeast**
½ cup	**warm water**
I cup	**unseasoned mashed potatoes**
2 cups	**warm milk**
½ cup	**shortening**
I cup	**sugar**
3	**eggs**
1½ teaspoons	**salt**
6 cups	**flour**
I small box	**chocolate instant pudding mix**
2 cups	**milk**
	vegetable oil, for frying
I container (16 ounces)	**chocolate frosting**

In a bowl, mix yeast, water, mashed potatoes, and milk together.

In a separate bowl, combine shortening, sugar, eggs, and salt. Stir mashed potato mixture into bowl with egg mixture. Stir in flour I cup at a time. Knead dough 1–2 minutes. Cover bowl with plastic wrap and allow dough to rise 45 minutes.

In a bowl, mix together pudding mix and milk until pudding thickens. Place in the refrigerator until ready to fill donuts.

Roll out dough to 1-inch thickness on a floured cutting board. Cut dough into 4 x 4-inch squares. Fry dough in hot oil. Turn once making sure donut is golden brown on both sides. Spread chocolate frosting over hot donuts and then fill donuts with chocolate pudding using a kitchen syringe. Refrigerate any leftovers. Makes 25–30 donuts.

CHOCOLATE GRAHAM CRACKER CAKE

2 small boxes	**chocolate instant pudding mix**
3 cups	**milk**
I container (8 ounces)	**frozen whipped topping,** thawed
I box (14 to 16 ounces)	**graham crackers**
I container (16 ounces)	**chocolate frosting**

In a 2-quart bowl, combine pudding and milk until smooth. Fold in whipped topping. Cover the bottom of a 9 x 13-inch pan with a layer of graham crackers, breaking to fit if necessary. Evenly spread half the pudding mixture over graham crackers. Lay another layer of crackers over pudding mixture. Spread remaining pudding over second graham cracker layer. Top with final layer of graham crackers. Melt chocolate frosting in the microwave 30 seconds. Stir and carefully drizzle chocolate frosting covering the entire cake. Cover and refrigerate a minimum of 3 hours before serving. Makes 20 servings.

VARIATIONS: Use vanilla, cheesecake, or white chocolate instant pudding mix in place of chocolate pudding mix.

TRIFLES & ENTERTAINING IDEAS

COOKIES-AND-CREAM TRIFLE

1	**chocolate or white cake mix**
	ingredients listed on back of box
2 small boxes	**chocolate instant pudding mix**
3 cups	**milk**
1 package (8 ounces)	**cream cheese,** softened
1 package (1 pound)	**chocolate sandwich cookies,** chopped
1 container (12 ounces)	**frozen whipped topping,** thawed

Make and bake cake according to package directions. Allow cake to cool and then crumble it. Mix together pudding mixes and milk and then beat in cream cheese.

In a glass punch bowl, layer half the cake crumbs, half the pudding mixture, and one-third of the cookies. Repeat layers with remaining cake crumbs, pudding mixture, and another third of the cookies. Spread whipped topping over top. Sprinkle remaining cookies over top. Refrigerate until ready to serve. Makes 24 servings.

MINT BROWNIE TRIFLE

1 (9 x 13-inch family size)	**brownie mix ingredients listed on back of box**
1 large box	**vanilla instant pudding mix**
3 cups	**milk**
1 package (18 ounces)	**mint chocolate cookies,** crushed
¹/₂ jar (11.75 ounces)	**hot fudge ice cream topping**
1 container (8 ounces)	**frozen whipped topping,** thawed

Prepare and bake brownies according to package directions in a greased 9 x 13-inch pan; cool completely and then cut into tiny squares.

In a bowl, mix pudding with milk until set. Pour half the pudding into the bottom of a large glass salad bowl or punch bowl. Place half the brownie squares evenly over pudding. Sprinkle one-third of the cookies over brownies. Drizzle half the ice cream topping over cookies. Repeat layers with remaining pudding, brownie squares, and another third of the cookie crumbs. Drizzle remaining ice cream topping over cookies and then spread whipped topping over top. To garnish, sprinkle remaining cookie crumbs over whipped topping. Makes 12–15 servings.

BUTTERFINGER BROWNIE A LA MODE

1 (8 x 8-inch size)	**brownie mix**
	ingredients listed on back of box
4	**Butterfinger candy bars,**
	chopped and divided
1/2 box (1/2 gallon)	**vanilla ice cream**
	chocolate syrup

Make brownie batter according to package directions. Stir half the chopped Butterfinger into batter. Bake brownies according to package directions. Place warm brownies on individual serving plates. Place a large scoop of vanilla ice cream over each brownie. Drizzle chocolate syrup over ice cream and then sprinkle with remaining Butterfingers. Makes 9 servings.

MINT CHOCOLATE CHIP BROWNIE SUNDAES

I (9 x 13-inch family size)	**brownie mix**
	ingredients listed on back of box
³/₄ cup	**mint chocolate chips**
	chocolate syrup
I box (¹/₂ gallon)	**mint chocolate chip ice cream**

Make brownie batter according to package directions. Stir chocolate chips into batter, and then bake as directed.

In separate serving bowls, drizzle syrup over bottom of dish and place a warm brownie over the syrup. Place one or two scoops of ice cream over top. Drizzle more syrup over ice cream. Serve immediately garnished with whipped topping and mint chocolate chips, if desired. Makes 20–24 servings.

VARIATION: For peanut butter sundaes, substitute peanut butter chips and peanut butter ice cream in place of the mint chocolate chips and ice cream.

CHOCOLATE LOVERS PARFAITS

1	**devil's food cake mix**
2	**eggs**
$^1/_2$ cup	**butter or margarine,** softened
1 cup	**semisweet chocolate chips**
2 small boxes	**chocolate instant pudding mix**
4 cups	**milk**
1 container (16 ounces)	**frozen whipped topping,** thawed
	grated chocolate bar, optional

Preheat oven to 350 degrees.

In a bowl, mix together cake mix, eggs, and butter; stir in chocolate chips. Mixture will be stiff. Press dough into a greased 9 x 13-inch pan. Bake 18 minutes. Allow to cool 1–2 hours and then crumble the cookie bars into a bowl.

In a separate bowl, stir pudding mix and milk together; chill 5 minutes. Layer cookie bar crumbs, pudding, and whipped topping in parfait glasses. Repeat with three layers. Sprinkle grated chocolate over the top of each parfait to garnish. Makes 12 large parfaits.

RASPBERRY BROWNIE CUPS

1 (9 x 13-inch family size)	**brownie mix**
	ingredients listed on back of box
2 squares (1-ounce each)	**white chocolate for baking**
2 tablespoons	**milk**
1 package (8 ounces)	**cream cheese,** softened
1/4 cup	**powdered sugar**
1 cup	**frozen whipped topping,** thawed
45 to 48	**raspberries**

Preheat oven to 325 degrees.

Make brownie batter according to package directions for cake-like brownies. Place a teaspoon of batter in each cup of a greased mini-muffin pan. Bake 14 minutes. Using a tart shaper or spoon, press down to form hollow brownie cups to hold filling.

In a bowl, melt chocolate and milk together 45–60 seconds in the microwave. Stir until chocolate is completely melted.

In a separate bowl, combine cream cheese and powdered sugar. Gradually stir in melted chocolate. Fold whipped topping into cream cheese mixture. Spoon cream cheese mixture into brownie cups. Place a raspberry on top of each brownie cup. Refrigerate 1–2 hours before serving. Makes 45–48 cups.

PEANUT BUTTER COOKIE CUPS

1 package (17.5 ounces)	**peanut butter cookie mix**
	ingredients listed on back of box
1 bag (12 ounces)	**miniature peanut butter cups**

Preheat oven to 350 degrees.

Make cookie dough according to package directions. Drop teaspoons of dough into cups of a greased mini-muffin pan. Press an unwrapped miniature peanut butter cup down into the center of each ball of dough until top of chocolate candy is even with top of cookie dough. Bake 8 minutes, or until lightly golden around the edges. Do not overcook. Remove from oven and allow cookies to set up in pan before removing. Makes 32 servings.

VARIATION: A chocolate chip cookie mix can be used in place of the peanut butter cookie mix.

PEANUT BUTTER CHOCOLATE LUSH

1	**chocolate cake mix**
1/2 cup	**butter or margarine,** melted
1	**egg**
2 small boxes	**chocolate instant pudding mix**
3 cups cold	**milk**

Peanut Butter Layer:

1/3 cup	**creamy peanut butter**
1/4 cup	**cold milk**
1 container (12 ounces)	**frozen whipped topping,** thawed
	unsalted peanuts
	chocolate syrup

Preheat oven to 350 degrees.

In a bowl, mix together cake mix, butter, and egg. Press dough to cover the bottom of a lightly greased 9 x 13-inch pan. Bake 14–16 minutes. With a fork, remove the air pockets by pushing down evenly over the entire hot crust; cool completely.

Beat together pudding mixes and milk with a wire whisk for 2 minutes. Spread evenly over cooled crust.

In a separate bowl, mix peanut butter and cold milk together with a wire whisk. Gently stir in the whipped topping; spread evenly over the chocolate layer. Chill 3–4 hours before serving. To garnish, sprinkle peanuts and drizzle chocolate syrup lightly over the top before serving. Makes 20 servings.

CHOCOLATE-DIPPED STRAWBERRIES

1 bag (11.5 ounces)	**semisweet or milk chocolate chips**
2 tablespoons	**shortening**
2 pounds	**fresh strawberries**

In a small slow cooker, melt chocolate chips with shortening on high heat. Turn heat to low.

Wash strawberries with leaves on. Place strawberries on a paper towel and softly blot dry. Dip strawberries in chocolate and then lay them on wax paper to dry. Or dip strawberries using a toothpick and turn strawberries upside down and insert toothpick into a piece of styrofoam to allow chocolate to dry. Makes 10–12 servings.

CHOCOLATE-
COVERED PRETZELS

I bag (11.5 ounces)	**semisweet or milk chocolate chips**
2 tablespoons	**shortening**
I bag (10 ounces)	**pretzel rods**
3	**Butterfinger candy bars,** crushed
I bag (8 ounces)	**toffee bits**

In a small slow cooker, melt chocolate chips with shortening on high heat. Turn heat to low. Dip pretzels in chocolate and then roll in Butterfingers or toffee bits or both. Lay them on wax paper to dry. Makes 10–12 servings.

VARIATION: Try rolling chocolate dipped pretzel in crushed candy canes for Christmas.

BERRY CHOCOLATE BARS

1 cup	**flour**
$^{1}/_{4}$ cup	**powdered sugar**
$^{1}/_{2}$ cup	**butter or margarine,** softened
$^{1}/_{2}$ cup	**strawberry, raspberry, or blueberry jam**
$^{1}/_{2}$ package (8 ounces)	**cream cheese,** softened
2 tablespoons	**milk**
1 cup	**white chocolate chips,** melted

Glaze:

$^{3}/_{4}$ cup	**semisweet chocolate chips**
1 tablespoon	**shortening**

Preheat oven to 375 degrees.

Mix flour and powdered sugar together. Cut butter into flour mixture until crumbly. Press mixture into a 9 x 9-inch pan. Bake 15–18 minutes, or until lightly brown; cool completely. Spread jam over crust.

In a small bowl, mix cream cheese and milk together. Mix in melted white chocolate until smooth. Spread cream cheese mixture over jam. Refrigerate 1 hour.

Melt chocolate chips and shortening together. Spread chocolate over bars. Chill another hour, or until ready to serve. Makes 16 bars.

CREAM PUFF SQUARES

I cup	**water**
1/2 cup	**butter or margarine**
I cup	**flour**
4	**eggs**
3 cups	**milk**
2 small boxes	**white chocolate instant pudding mix**
I package (8 ounces)	**cream cheese,** softened
I container (12 ounces)	**frozen whipped topping,** thawed **chocolate syrup**

Preheat oven to 400 degrees.

In a 2-quart pan, bring water and butter to a boil. Stir in flour until mixture forms a ball; remove from heat. Beat in eggs one at a time until smooth. Spread dough into a greased baking sheet. Bake 25–28 minutes, or until golden brown; cool completely.

In a 2-quart bowl, beat milk and pudding mixes together. Beat cream cheese into pudding mixture. Spread pudding mixture over cooled crust. Spread whipped topping over pudding. Drizzle chocolate syrup decoratively over the top. Makes 24–28 squares.

NOTES

Metric Conversion Chart

Liquid and Dry Measures

U.S.	Canadian	Australian
¼ teaspoon	1 mL	1 ml
½ teaspoon	2 mL	2 ml
1 teaspoon	5 mL	5 ml
1 tablespoon	15 mL	20 ml
¼ cup	50 mL	60 ml
⅓ cup	75 mL	80 ml
½ cup	125 mL	125 ml
⅔ cup	150 mL	170 ml
¾ cup	175 mL	190 ml
1 cup	250 mL	250 ml
1 quart	1 liter	1 litre

Temperature Conversion Chart

Fahrenheit	Celsius
250	120
275	140
300	150
325	160
350	180
375	190
400	200
425	220
450	230
475	240
500	260

Yum!

Each 128 pages, $9.95

ABOUT THE AUTHOR

Stephanie Ashcraft, author of the original *101 Things To Do With A Cake Mix*, has taught cooking classes based on the tips and meals in her cookbooks for almost ten years. She lives in Tucson, Arizona, with her husband and four children. Samples from this book have made her a favorite neighbor in her community. Stephanie, a native of Kirklin, Indiana, graduated from Brigham Young University with a degree in family science. This is her 12th cookbook.

$9.99 U.S.

101 Things To Do With Chocolate

101 Things To Do With Chocolate gives you an endless supply of chocolate fixes for special occasions and every day. Satisfy your chocolate cravings with these easy recipes.

Brownie Ice Cream Cake
Decadent Chocolate Truffles
Chocolate Mint Layer Brownies
Chocolate Pudding-Filled Donuts
And more!

Cookbook

ISBN-13: 978-1-4236-0180-7
ISBN-10: 1-4236-0180-7

50999

9 781423 601807

Gibbs Smith, Publisher